What
The Holy BIBLE Says
About
Light

Fran Rogers

And God said, "Let there be light,"
and there was light. "
And God saw that the light was good.
Genesis 1:3-4

What the Holy BIBLE Says about LIGHT
<u>1st Edition</u>

© 2016 Fran Rogers
Father and Family Books

ISBN-13:978-0692680490
ISBN-10:0692680497

fatherandfamily.com
godsgracegodsglory.com

Unless otherwise indicated Scripture quotations are
from The Holy Bible, King James Version

Dedicated to our daughter, Lee Ellen,
through whom God's light shines
and makes her a delight to others

Contents

INTRODUCTION

This first book in the series *What the Holy Bible Says,* springs from my joy of plunging into God's Word, with a passion to know what He, the Giver of Life, says about life ~ all of life. It started with one word, and evolved to develop and reveal many words that together form the thoughts and images that God wants us to have.

LIGHT was the first word chosen from a book I had written on addictions. That study was intended to show how we all live in darkness until God reveals His light in our hearts and lives. We used four subjects of that yearlong study and are now publishing each of them separately. As we study the subject of *light* from God's Word He shines His light into our hearts, reveals its true meaning, and the power that is in His light. Just as He said in the beginning when He created the heavens and the earth, "Let there be light, and there was light" so that same light shines through His written word, giving us that same power to change our darkness into light. As His Spirit moved across the face of the waters so, from His Word, His Spirit moves in us to give us light, filling our darkness and making us light in the darkness of this world.

That you may be blameless and innocent, children of God without blemish in the midst of a crooked and twisted generation, among whom you shine as lights in the world, that you may be blameless and innocent, children of God without blemish in the midst of a crooked and twisted generation, among whom you shine as lights in the world. Philippians 2:15

This ten-week study can be an individual study or a group study. The amount of time for each day's devotion depends on the individual and how much he/she wants to retain of what they are reading.

It is simple, and straightforward from God's Word, The Holy Bible. In the use of *Strong's Concordance* for the King James Version, we have listed the references for daily study and meditation, with a review and evaluation at the end of each week.

Along with this and other studies I recommend reading *The Garden of GOD'S WORD ~ The Purpose and Delight of BIBLE STUDY*, second of the series *Little Books About the Magnitude of God.*

I pray that your heart be enlightened and lifted in praise, adoration, and joy to the God of *light that shines into our hearts the knowledge of the glory of God in the face of Jesus Christ*; that your light may shine and glorify your Father in heaven.

Fran Rogers   2016

WEEK 1
Genesis 1 ~ Psalm 36

❧ DAY 1

READ Genesis 1:1-5

What are the contrasts?

Which has the preeminence?

Who is in control of the *light, the days and the nights?*

Our Father in heaven, hallowed be Thy name. Thy kingdom come, Thy will be done on earth, in my heart and my life, today. In Jesus name I pray. Amen

---

❧ DAY 2

REVIEW Genesis 1:1-5

READ AND COMPARE
Revelation 21:10-11, 22-22:5

Where does the *light* originate? Vs.11

Who is the *light?* Vs. 23

Where is the night and darkness? Vs.5

Pray that He would be the light of your life.

🕮 DAY 3

READ EXODUS 13:17-22

*And the LORD went before them by day in a pillar of a cloud,
to lead them the way; and by night in a pillar of fire,
to give them light;
to go by day and night:* vs.21

What is the purpose of the light?

Pray for His leading in your heart and life.

🕮 DAY 4

READ 2 Chronicles 21: 1-7

*Howbeit the LORD would not destroy the house of David,
because of the covenant that he had made with David,
and as he promised to give a light to him and to his sons for ever.*
Vs. 7

Who is in control of the light?

Ask for this light for you and your family.

❧ DAY 5

READ Job 33:14-30

He will deliver his soul from going into the pit,
and his life shall see the light.
Lo, all these things worketh God oftentimes with man,
To bring back his soul from the pit,
to be enlightened with the light of the living.
vs. 28-30

What is the purpose of the light in these verses?

Pray for His light for deliverance.

❧ DAY 6

READ Psalm 27: 1-14

The LORD is my light and my salvation; whom shall I fear?
The LORD is the strength of my life;
of whom shall I be afraid? vs. 1

Look for the word "heart" and the LORD's work of
salvation.

Pray for His saving work.

DAY 7

READ Psalm 36:5-12

For with thee is the fountain of life:
in thy light shall we see light. Vs.9

In these verses meditate on God's character.

Pray for His light.

Thoughts From Week 1

Record and meditate on the main thoughts about *light* from this past week---its source, purpose, comparisons, etc. Pray according to what you have learned about the *light*.

WEEK 2
Psalm 37 ~ Psalm 104

✥ DAY 8

READ Psalm 37:1-23

And he shall bring forth thy righteousness as the light,
and thy judgment as the noonday. Vs. 6

How would you describe righteousness from these verses?

Ask for His righteousness.
_____

✥ DAY 9

READ Psalm 43:1-5

O send out thy light and thy truth: let them lead me;
let them bring me unto thy holy hill, and to thy tabernacles.
Vs. 3

What is the result of His light in these verses?

Pray for His light to lead you.

✿ DAY 10

READ Psalm 44:1-8

*For they got not the land in possession by their own sword,
neither did their own arm save them: but thy right hand,
and thine arm, and the light of thy countenance,
because thou hadst a favour unto them.* Vs. 3

What was God's work and His title in this Psalm?

Pray for His power and presence.

✿ DAY 11

READ Psalm 56:1-13

*For thou hast delivered my soul from death:
wilt not thou deliver my feet from falling,
as I may walk before God in the light of the living?* vs. 13

What does this Psalm testify of God?

Pray that you may walk before God in His light.

🦋 DAY 12

READ Psalm 89:1-26

"Blessed is the people that know the joyful sound:
they shall walk, O LORD, in the light of thy countenance."
Vs. 15

What are the LORD's characteristics in this Psalm?

What are His names?

Pray for the joyful sound.
_____

🦋 DAY 13

READ Psalm 97:1-12

Light is sown for the righteous,
and gladness for the upright in heart. Vs. 11

What does the LORD do?

What do His hands do?

Pray for a fertile heart.

🐾 DAY 14

READ Psalm104:1-35

Who coverest thyself with light as with a garment:
who stretchest out the heavens like a curtain: vs. 2

In His light meditate on His majesty and His rule over
all things.

Ask for His rule in you.

🐾 Thoughts from Week 2

Review and record from this past week what you have
learned about God's character, His names, His work,
and the believer's response to His light.

Pray according to what you have learned

WEEK 3
Psalm 112 ~ Proverbs 6

DAY 15

READ Psalm 112:1-10

Unto the upright there ariseth light in the darkness:
he is gracious, and full of compassion, and righteous.
Vs.4

What is characteristic of those who fear the LORD?

Ask for light in your darkness.

DAY 16

READ Psalm 118:1-29

God is the LORD, which hath showed us light:
bind the sacrifice with cords, even unto the horns of the altar.
Vs.27

Meditate on why we should give thanks to the LORD.

Praise Him for showing us light.

🦋 DAY 17

READ Psalm 119: 105-112

Thy word is a lamp unto my feet,
and a light unto my path.
Vs. 105

How does God give us His light?

Praise Him for His holy word.

🦋 DAY 18

READ Psalm 119:129-136

The entrance of thy words giveth light;
it giveth understanding unto the simple. Vs. 130

Which comes first---His word or His light?

Ask Him to speak through His word to you.

🕮 DAY 19

READ Psalm 139:1-24

*If I say, Surely the darkness shall cover me;
even the night shall be light about me." Vs. 1
Yea, the darkness hideth not from thee;
but the night shineth as the day:
the darkness and the light are both alike to thee.* Vs. 12

Is anything hidden from God?

Meditate and pray through this Psalm.

_____

🕮 DAY 20

READ Proverbs 4:1-27

*But the path of the just is as the shining light,
that shineth more and more unto the perfect day.* Vs. 18

To what is light compared and where is it kept?

Ask Him to keep you on the right path.

🕮 DAY 21

READ Proverbs 6:1-24

For the commandment is a lamp; and the law is light;
and reproofs of instruction are the way of life. vs. 23

Meditate on vs. 20-23.

Pray that His word would become law in your heart
and life.

🕮 Thoughts from Week 3

From this week's readings and meditation in light of
God's Word, what should we thank and praise the
LORD for?

What should we pray for?

WEEK 4
Proverbs 13 ~ Isaiah 8

✱ DAY 22

READ Proverbs 13:1-25

The light of the righteous rejoiceth;
but the lamp of the wicked shall be put out. Vs. 9

Compare the life of the wise and the wicked?

Pray for this continual rejoicing.

_____

✱ DAY 23

READ Ecclesiastes 2:1-15

Then I saw that wisdom excelleth folly,
as far as light excelleth darkness
The wise man's eyes are in his head;
but the fool walketh in darkness:
and I myself perceived also
that one event happeneth to them all. Vs. 13, 14

What did the wise man continue to say in his heart?

Pray that you walk in the light.

🕮 DAY 24

READ Ecclesiastes 11: 1-10

Truly the light is sweet,
and a pleasant thing it is for the eyes to behold the sun:
But if a man live many years, and rejoice in them all;
yet let him remember the days of darkness;
for they shall be many.
All that cometh is vanity. Vs. 7,8

What is the light of wisdom in Ecclesiastes 11:10?

Pray to put away what is evil and vain.

_____

🕮 DAY 25

READ Ecclesiastes 12:1-14

While the sun, or the light, or the moon, or the stars, be not darkened,
nor the clouds return after the rain: In the day when the keepers of the
house shall tremble, and the strong men shall bow themselves, and the
grinders cease because they are few, and those that look out of the
windows be darkened, Vs. 2,3

What was "the conclusion of the whole matter?"

Pray that you keep His commandments

🕊 DAY 26

READ Isaiah 2: 1-22

O house of Jacob, come ye,
and let us walk in the light of the LORD. Vs. 5

Compare the darkness of man to the light of the
LORD.

Pray to walk in His light.

_____

🕊 DAY 27

READ Isaiah 5: 1-30

Woe unto them that call evil good, and good evil;
that put darkness for light, and light for darkness;
that put bitter for sweet, and sweet for bitter! Vs. 20

What is revealed about a person who has no light or
knowledge?

Pray for knowledge.

🕮 DAY 28

READ Isaiah 8:1-22

To the law and to the testimony:
if they speak not according to this word,
it is because there is no light in them. Vs. 20

Where is our sanctuary in the middle of the darkness?

Pray for His light in you.

🕮 Thoughts from Week 4

In the comparison of wisdom and wickedness, light and darkness, where is our only hope for wisdom, light, and life?

Is what we desire in our hearts according to what we think God wants for us, or according to what His light reveals to us?

Pray according to your true needs.

WEEK 5
Isaiah 9 ~ Isaiah 58

✂ DAY 29

READ Isaiah 9:1-8

*The people that walked in darkness have seen a great light:
they that dwell in the land of the shadow of death,
upon them hath the light shined.* Vs.2

How does Isaiah describe the light?

Of whom and under whom?

Pray for great light.

✂ DAY 30

READ Isaiah 10:16-27

*And the light of Israel shall be for a fire,
and his Holy One for a flame:
and it shall burn and devour his thorns and briers in one day;.*
Vs. 17

To what is His light compared?

Pray for this fire in you.

🎕 DAY 31

READ Isaiah 42:1-16

I the LORD have called thee in righteousness,
and will hold thine hand, and will keep thee,
and give thee for a covenant of the people
for a light of the Gentiles; vs. 6

What is the response to the light?

Pray for these new paths.

🎕 DAY 32

READ Isaiah 49:1-18

And he said, It is a light thing that thou shouldest be my
servant to raise up the tribes of Jacob
and to restore the preserved of Israel:
I will also give thee for a light to the Gentiles, that thou mayest
be my salvation unto the end of the earth. Vs. 6

Meditate on the promises in verses 8-10 & 15-17.

Pray that He would make you a light to others.

🦋 DAY 33

READ Isaiah 50:1-11

Who is among you that feareth the LORD,
that obeyeth the voice of his servant,
that walketh in darkness, and hath no light?
let him trust in the name of the LORD,
and stay upon his God. Vs. 10

Meditate on and pray for the power of the LORD
mentioned in this chapter.

🦋 DAY 34

READ Isaiah 51:1-16

Hearken unto me, my people;
and give ear unto me, O my nation:
for a law shall proceed from me,
and I will make my judgment to rest for a light of the people.
Vs. 4

Compare and pray for what God promises and what
He expects from His people.

✿ DAY 35

READ Isaiah 58:1-14

Then shall thy light break forth as the morning,
and thine health shall spring forth speedily:
and thy righteousness shall go before thee;
the glory of the LORD shall be thy rereward. Vs. 8

What is the proof of light in us---toward man and
toward God?

Pray for this.

✿ Thoughts from Week 5

In what forms was the light revealed, and what effect
does God's light have on His people.

Pray for the power of His light in your heart and life;
to shine through you for His glory.

WEEK 6
Isaiah 59 ~ Matthew

🎵 DAY 36

READ Isaiah 59:1-21

Therefore is judgment far from us,
neither doth justice overtake us:
we wait for light, but behold obscurity;
for brightness, but we walk in darkness. Vs.9

What keeps us from the light of God?

What is our hope?

Pray for His judgment and mercy.

🎵 DAY 37

READ Isaiah 60:1-22

And the Gentiles shall come to thy light,
and kings to the brightness of thy rising. Vs. 3

The sun shall be no more thy light by day; neither for brightness shall
the moon give light unto thee: but the LORD shall be unto thee an
everlasting light, and thy God thy glory. Thy sun shall no more go
down; neither shall thy moon withdraw itself: for the LORD shall be
thine everlasting light, and the days of thy mourning shall be ended.:
Vs. 19, 20

What effect and to what purpose is light in this chapter?

Pray for His drawing.

❧ DAY 38

READ Jeremiah 13:15-27

Give glory to the LORD your God, before he cause darkness,
and before your feet stumble upon the dark mountains,
and, while ye look for light,
he turn it into the shadow of death, and make it gross darkness.
Vs. 16

What are the LORD's instructions?

Pray that you will hear and be humbled.

❧ DAY 39

READ Hosea 6:1-11

Therefore have I hewed them by the prophets;
I have slain them by the words of my mouth:
and thy judgments are as the light that goeth forth. Vs. 5

What does the light require? Vs. 6

To what does the light refer?

Pray for knowledge to follow on.

❧ DAY 40

READ Micah 7:1-20

Rejoice not against me, O mine enemy: when I fall, I shall arise; when I sit in darkness, the LORD shall be a light unto me. I will bear the indignation of the LORD, because I have sinned against him, until he plead my cause, and execute judgment for me: he will bring me forth to the light, and I shall behold his righteousness. Vs. 8,9

Meditate on this passage of scripture and pray for the light of His righteousness.

———————————————————————

❧ DAY 41

READ Habakkuk 3:1-18

And his brightness was as the light;
he had horns coming out of his hand:
and there was the hiding of his power."
Vs. 4

How is the light described?

Pray for His salvation and strength.

🕮 DAY 42

READ Matthew 4:11-17

The people which sat in darkness saw great light;
and to them which sat in the region and shadow of death
light is sprung up Vs. 16.

In and through whom has the *great light* come?

Pray for repentance.

🕮 Thoughts from Week 6

We began the week learning that sin separates us from God and His light. Where does He, in His light, bring us?

Follow through and pray again for what you find and need.

WEEK 7
Matthew 5 ~ John 5

✎ DAY 43

READ Matthew 5:1-20

"Ye are the light of the world. A city that is set on an
hill cannot be hid. Neither do men light a candle, and
put it under a bushel, but on a candlestick; and it
giveth light unto all that are in the house. Let your
light so shine before men, that they may see your good
works, and glorify your Father which is in heaven."
Vs. 14,15,16

What does the light reveal as the character of those in
the kingdom of heaven?

Pray for His righteousness.

✎ DAY 44

READ Luke 1:67-80

*To give light to them that sit in darkness
and in the shadow of death,
to guide our feet into the way of peace.* Vs.79

What does the light reveal in these verses?

Pray for this.

DAY 45

READ Luke 2:21-40

A light to lighten the Gentiles, and the glory of thy people Israel.
Vs. 32

Give thanks to the Lord for what the light revealed to Simeon and Anna. Vs. 30, 38

DAY 46

READ Luke 11:29-36

"The light of the body is the eye: therefore when thine eye is single, thy whole body also is full of light; but when thine eye is evil, thy body also is full of darkness. Take heed therefore that the light which is in thee be not darkness. If thy whole body therefore be full of light, having no part dark, the whole shall be full of light, as when the bright shining of a candle doth give thee light." Vs. 34,35,36

What is Jesus revealing about Himself?

Pray that you not be deceived but have full light.

🕮 DAY 47

READ John 1:1-18

In him was life; and the life was the light of men.
And the light shineth in darkness;
and the darkness comprehended it not.

The same came for a witness, to bear witness of the Light,
that all men through him might believe. He was not that Light,
but was sent to bear witness of that Light.
That was the true Light, which lighteth every man that cometh
into the world. Vs. 4,5,7,9

Who is the light?

What comes to us through Him?

Pray for these.

🕮 DAY 48

READ John 3:1-21

"And this is the condemnation, that light is come into the
world, and men loved darkness rather than light, because
their deeds were evil. For every one that doeth evil hateth
the light, neither cometh to the light, lest his deeds should
be reproved. But he that doeth truth cometh to the light,
that his deeds may be made manifest, that they are wrought
in God." Vs.19, 20, 21
What is the proof of the truth?

Pray that you would love the light.

❧ DAY 49

READ John 5:20-36

He was a burning and a shining light:
and ye were willing for a season to rejoice in his light.
Vs. 35

Why was Jesus' light, works, and witness greater than
John's?

Pray to rejoice in His light.

❧ Thoughts from Week 7

We pray that at the end of these seven weeks you have
come to a special place in your relationship with God,
the Father, and the Lord Jesus Christ. Plan a special
time between you and the Lord, to pray and meditate
on this past week's Bible references. They should be
powerful in His light to reveal Jesus Christ as the light
of your life. This may be a time to reevaluate your
heart's commitment to Him. Record here any special
thoughts on these past weeks.

Pray for His will and the power of the Holy Spirit in
your plans and goals.

WEEK 8
John 8 ~ 2 Corinthians 4

🕮 DAY 50

READ John 8:12-36

Then spake Jesus again unto them, saying,
"I am the light of the world:
he that followeth me shall not walk in darkness,
but shall have the light of life." Vs. 12

What are the contrasts between Jesus and the
Pharisees?

Pray for light to follow Jesus.

_____

🕮 DAY 51

READ John 12:23-36

Then Jesus said unto them, "Yet a little while is the light with
you. Walk while ye have the light, lest darkness come upon
you: for he that walketh in darkness knoweth not whither
he goeth. While ye have light, believe in the light, that ye
may be the children of light. These things spake Jesus, and
departed, and did hide himself from them." Vs. 35, 36

What are the three things Jesus says we must do?
Vs. 26, 35, 36

❧ DAY 52

READ John 12:37-50

"I am come a light into the world,
that whosoever believeth on me
should not abide in darkness."
Vs. 46

What is the proof that we do not abide in *darkness*?
Vs. 36, 46

❧ DAY 53

READ Acts 13:44-52

*For so hath the Lord commanded us,
saying, I have set thee to be a light of the Gentiles,
that thou shouldest be for salvation unto the ends of the earth.*
Vs. 47

Why was Paul set to be *a light to the Gentiles?*

Pray for the Holy Spirit in your life.

🕮 DAY 54

READ Acts 26:1-20

At midday, O king, I saw in the way a light from heaven,
above the brightness of the sun, shining round about m
and them which journeyed with me. Vs. 13

"To open their eyes, and to turn them from darkness to light, and from the power of Satan unto God, that they may receive forgiveness of sins, and inheritance among them which are sanctified by faith that is in me." *Vs. 18*

"That Christ should suffer,
and that he should be the first that should rise from the dead,
and should show light unto the people, and to the Gentiles." Vs. 23

Who was the light that appeared to Paul?

For what purpose did he appear to Paul?   17-20

🕮 DAY 55

READ Romans 13:8-14

The night is far spent, the day is at hand: let us therefore cast off
the works of darkness, and let us put on the armour of light.
But put ye on the Lord Jesus Christ,
and make not provision for the flesh,
to fulfil the lusts thereof. Vs. 12, 14

Who is this armour of light?

What should you pray for today?

🕮 DAY 56

READ 2 Corinthians 4:1-7

In whom the god of this world hath blinded the minds of them which believe not, lest the light of the glorious gospel of Christ, who is the image of God, should shine unto them. For God, who commanded the light to shine out of darkness, hath shined in our hearts, to give the light of the knowledge of the glory of God in the face of Jesus Christ. Vs. 4,6

How is the light described?

Pray for the fullness of this treasure in your heart.

🕮 Thoughts from Week 8

What difference has Christ made in your life this past week?

How have you been tested in your faith as it concerns earthly desire of the flesh?

Pray for more faith with the understanding that it is His light---the *excellency of His light and His power* working in you. Pray that you not be *blinded by the god of this world*; that the *glorious gospel of Christ* would shine in your heart and through you---that seeing Christ the Lord, you would be *changed into His image from glory to glory.* Keep reading. Meditate on His Word. Be filled with the joy, the Holy Spirit and praise for His light and glory.

"To learn Christ is to be made like Christ, to have the divine characters of his holiness engraven upon our hearts: "we all with open face, beholding as in a glass the glory of the Lord, are changed into the same image." 2 Cor. 3. 18 There is a metamorphosis made; a sinner, viewing Christ's image in the glass of the gospel, is transformed into that image. Never did any man look upon Christ with a spiritual eye, but he went away quite changed. A true saint is a divine landscape picture, where all the rare beauties of Christ are lively portrayed and drawn forth; he hath the same spirit, the same judgment, the same will, with Jesus Christ."

Thomas Watson (1620-1686)

WEEK 9
2 Corinthians 6 ~ 1 Peter 2

🎗 DAY 57

READ 2 Corinthians 6:1-18

*Be ye not unequally yoked together with unbelievers: for what
fellowship hath righteousness with unrighteousness?
and what communion hath light with darkness?* Vs. 14

What is synonymous with light in vs. 1, 14, 15, 18?

Pray for vs. 17.

_____

🎗 DAY 58

READ 2 Corinthians 11:1-15

*And no marvel;
for Satan himself is transformed into an angel of light.* Vs. 14

How is it possible to be deceived? Vs. 3, 13-15

Pray for *the simplicity that is in Christ.*

DAY 59

READ Ephesians 5:1-20

For ye were sometimes darkness,
but now are ye light in the Lord: walk as children of light.
Vs. 8
But all things that are reproved are made manifest by the light:
for whatsoever doth make manifest is light. Wherefore he saith,
Awake thou that sleepest, and arise from the dead,
and Christ shall give thee light. Vs. 13,14

Based on today's reading what should you pray for?

DAY 60

READ Colossians 1:1-29

Giving thanks unto the Father,
which hath made us meet to be
partakers of the inheritance of the saints in light:
Who hath delivered us from the power of darkness,
and hath translated us into the kingdom of his dear Son:
Vs. 12, 13

What does the Father do? Vs. 12-13.

Why do we pray to *be filled with the knowledge of His will in all wisdom and spiritual understanding*? Vs. 10-11

🎜 DAY 61

READ 1 Thessalonians 5:1-24

But ye, brethren, are not in darkness,
that that day should overtake you as a thief.
Ye are all the children of light, and the children of the day:
we are not of the night, nor of darkness. Vs. 4,5

From this chapter describe the *children of light.*

Pray for this in your own life.

_____

🎜 DAY 62

READ 2 Timothy 1:1-14

But is now made manifest by the appearing of our
Saviour Jesus Christ,
who hath abolished death,
and hath brought life and immortality to light
through the gospel: Vs. 10

What is revealed by the light? Vs. 1,9,10

In whom is this life?

Pray in light of vs.13,14.

✨ DAY 63

READ 1 Peter 2:1-12

But ye are a chosen generation, a royal priesthood,
an holy nation, a peculiar people;
that ye should show forth the praises of him
who hath called you out of darkness into his marvellous light.
vs. 9

Describe those who are called out of darkness.

Pray that this is a description of you.

✨ Thoughts from Week 9

Do you see yourself any differently, in light of what you have learned this week? Do you see yourself as one of the Father's *children of light?* Have you gained more hours of light for His glory? Record how He has been working in your heart this week.

Pray fervently for His Holy Spirit to work in you for this last week in the study of light and how it affects your heart and life.

WEEK 10
2 Peter 1 ~ Revelation 22

✾ DAY 64

READ 2 Peter 1:1-21

We have also a more sure word of prophecy;
whereunto ye do well that ye take heed,
as unto a light that shineth in a dark place, until the day dawn,
and the day star arise in your hearts: Vs. 19

Meditate on this chapter and pray for what you find in each verse.

✾ DAY 65

READ 1 John 1:1-10

This then is the message which we have heard of him,
and declare unto you,
that God is light, and in him is no darkness at all.
But if we walk in the light, as he is in the light,
we have fellowship one with another,
and the blood of Jesus Christ his Son cleanseth us from all sin.
Vs. 7

With whom is our fellowship of light?

Pray for full cleansing.

✿ DAY 66

READ 1 John 2:1-17

"Again, a new commandment I write unto you, which thing is true in him and in you: because the darkness is past, and the true light now shineth. He that saith he is in the light, and hateth his brother, is in darkness even until now. He that loveth his brother abideth in the light, and there is none occasion of stumbling in him. But he that hateth his brother is in darkness, and walketh in darkness, and knoweth not whither he goeth, because that darkness hath blinded his eyes."
Vs. 8,9,10,11

What is the proof of abiding in the light?

Pray for your loving and abiding.

🦋 DAY 67

READ Revelation 21:1-21

Having the glory of God:
and her light was like unto a stone most precious,
even like a jasper stone, clear as crystal;
I saw no temple therein: for the Lord God Almighty
and the Lamb are the temple of it."
And the city had no need of the sun,
neither of the moon, to shine in it:
for the glory of God did lighten it,
and the Lamb is the light thereof.
And the nations of them which are saved
shall walk in the light of it:
and the kings of the earth do bring their glory
and honour into it.
vs. 11,23,24

Meditate on this chapter.

Who will *inherit all things* in the new heaven and earth?

DAY 68

READ Revelation 22:1-20

And there shall be no night there; and they need no candle, neither light of the sun; for the Lord God giveth them light: and they shall reign for ever and ever. Vs. 5

Where did the light begin? (Genesis 1)

What is the end result of God's light? (Revelation 22)

Record what you have learned from what the Bible says about light, what you understand, how you relate and respond to the light that the Bible reveals.

NOTES

About the Author

Fran Rogers is a wife/caregiver to her husband of 55 years, a 77-year-old great-grandmother, writer and blogger in Buford, Georgia. She writes from the experience of enduring many difficulties while living in the reality of God's grace. Through God's Word she has learned to be dependent on Him for all things, witnessing His love, joy, and goodness. Writing for over twenty-five years, she is now beginning to publish what God has been teaching her. The purpose of publishing is to share with God's people the legacy of His kingdom. She is a witness of God's provisions for all things of this life, and even more; the eternal life that He has prepared for all His people. The majority of proceeds from sales will be given to charity and to missions that witness of God's kingdom throughout this world. In view of Christ's promise that He would have witnesses in *Jerusalem, Judea, and Samaria, and to the uttermost part of the earth,* her hope is that God's people who read will not only benefit, but also promote this message to others through their purchase. See the website fatherandfamily.com for more details of this ministry.

Other books are available, or soon to be published, in this series and the series *Little Books About the Magnitude of God*; her work is longer than an article, but not as extensive as a regular length book.

Thank you for purchasing this book. Please consider leaving a review online.

✿ FREE EBOOKS

FIRST THINGS That Last FOREVER
fatherandfamily.com

Sign up for a second free eBook

TWO FULL PLATES ~ *Learning to be a Caregiver*

www.fatherandfamily.com/free-eBook/

Website: fatherandfamily.com
Blog: godsgracegodsglory.com
Facebook: Father and Family Books
Contact: contact@fatherandfamily.com

Other Books in Series